FAITH IN JESUS CHRIST

JOHN COVENTRY, S.J.

Darton, Longman and Todd
London

First published in Great Britain in 1980
Darton, Longman & Todd Ltd
89 Lillie Road
London SW6 1UD

ISBN 0 232 51474 7

In general biblical quotations are from the Revised Standard Version of the Bible, copyright 1952 and 1971 by the Division of Christian Education of the National Council of the Churches of Christ in the U.S.A.

Printed in Great Britain by
Richard Clay (The Chaucer Press) Ltd
Bungay, Suffolk

Practical Theology Series

Editors' Introduction

The Vatican Council ended in 1965. It ratified for the whole Catholic Church a policy of living the Christian life in closer touch with the perspectives of the Bible: love more than law, community more than hierarchy, affirmation of the world more than distrust, the unique worth of the individual more than uniformity.

The Church has now had fifteen years of experience of these principles: of the hope they bring, the problems and opportunities of implementing them, and above all our need of them as we face the challenges of the future.

Written for the ordinary Catholic, this series describes where we have got to. It recalls that magnificent view of God's relationship with his people in the world of today and what we have so far done about establishing his Kingdom. It tries to see the implications of all this for the decisions we have to make today as individual Catholics who are members of his Church.

Edmund Flood, O.S.B.
John Coventry, S.J.

CONTENTS

1

THE GROUND UNDER OUR FEET

It is a common experience for a Christian, who has thought out his beliefs and fitted them together coherently, to read or hear something one day which casts doubt on some central piece in the pattern, with the result that the whole structure suddenly seems shaky. It is an unnerving experience: the temptation is to run away, to refuse to look more closely. However, it is an equally common experience that, if you face up to the difficulty and think things through, you emerge from what may well have been a time of trial into a deeper and more satisfying grasp of the belief in question, and probably a deeper appreciation of your Christian faith as a whole. When it has happened a number of times,,you are less unnerved at a new challenge, more confident in the power of faith to enlighten and to satisfy your God-given power of understanding. On reflection, neither the unnerving nor the eventual reinforcing should surprise us. We cannot insulate our faith; if we develop our education and our understanding in many other areas of human life, our beliefs will need to keep up, to grow up, to live at peace in the same house with our other ideas. Indeed, we *should* not insulate our beliefs: faith of its nature 'seeks understanding'; and we should welcome the power of Jesus Christ to bring us light.

Many different kinds of book could be written about faith in Jesus Christ. This one has been written in the hope that it will bring some help and assurance to those faced with one of today's great challenges, the anxieties that arise for many from modern study of the New Testament. Many Christians, and among them many clergy who have to preach Sunday by Sunday, have to a greater or lesser extent become aware that they can no longer take the Gospels entirely at their face value as simple recordings of what happened. This can cause us great uneasiness, anxiety; there can be the feeling that the ground is taken away from under our feet, and we may begin to be unsure what our faith and its characteristic beliefs really rest on.

When we study the Gospels more closely, we come to realize that they grew, developed, got put into different shapes, in the early Church. They are not, as they stand, straightforward records of how Jesus appeared to anybody during his lifetime. They are, through and through, the product over a number of years of a Church which believed in the resurrection and the lordship of Christ, a Church which saw Jesus' lifetime through the filter of these later beliefs, of this later vision, a Church which shaped and reshaped its material about Jesus both in the light of later meditations on Jesus' words and actions, and in the light of their own needs as Christian communities in different parts of the Roman world. We can come to appreciate the Gospels as giving a marvellous insight into the life and faith of the growing Church, but we begin to wonder to what extent they give us a reliable picture of Jesus. There could, of course, be no such thing as a 'factual' picture of Jesus (or anyone else) which was not a record of his impact on particular persons; the point is, rather, that these records are heavily overlaid with later faith and devotion. The suspicion may creep into our minds that Christians got carried away by enthusiasm into elaborating and embroidering their own and other people's memories of Jesus. If so, where do we stand? Does our faith depend on recovering from the texts a more contemporary picture of what Jesus said and did and what it meant to people at the time? Or does it rest on the New Testament precisely as a witness to the faith of the Church which believed in the resurrection and lordship of Christ? Or does it, perhaps, not ultimately rest on the New Testament at all?

The resurrection itself is at the centre of the disquiet caused by today's study of Scripture, as is obvious to any who have come across the works of contemporary writers in this field, whether Catholic or Anglican or Lutheran or others. It is not a matter of taking sides as between Churches, but of what one can learn by studying the documents by modern historical methods, and what one cannot. The first people to proclaim the resurrection of Jesus had all been his followers. Might it not be more convincing, if he had appeared to some who did not believe in him or had even opposed him? Someone like Caiaphas? Did the first witnesses to the resurrection somehow work themselves up into imagining that Jesus still lived and had appeared to them? And if such a suggestion is so disquieting that one feels the rug is being pulled out from under Christian faith, then what means are there of refuting it? Of course, Paul claimed that the risen Jesus had appeared to him, and he had not been a disciple: far from it; he had persecuted the Church. But Paul's testimony does not solve the problem by itself, immensely valuable though it is. He was not one of those who originated faith in the risen Lord. The Christian community had by the time of his conversion existed for two or three years and had gathered force and shape. God specially chose him to expound and spread the faith, but we cannot say that it would have collapsed without him. Paul is a most valuable witness in many ways, and we shall need to consider him more fully. But he is not a sufficient witness. Like the first witnesses he claimed that he had seen the Lord, and his faith is based on that: he does not mention the empty tomb. Like us he was not a follower of the historical Jesus, but joined an already existing community of faith.

Finally, present-day understanding of the New Testament forces us to look hard at the question of the divinity of Christ. Modern thought and scholarship are characterized by a historical sense. Our forbears could happily treat all the New Testament writings as if they had been penned by individuals among Jesus' followers who knew one another, had a clear memory of what Jesus said and did (with the very large exception of Paul), and were fully in touch with one another as they set it all down within a comparatively short time. Roughly, Christians treated any part of the New Testament as contemporary with any other, and set about building a composite picture by harmonizing the different narratives and ways of thinking as well as they could. Today we realize that we have documents which in their present form span at least forty and perhaps as much as seventy years of developing practice, developing life, developing thought, in different parts of a small but diversified world. This gives us the fascinating task and opportunity of laying out, at least in broad outlines, the history of early Christian life and thought; the chance to disentangle the earlier from the later and to become spectators of the whole process of Christian growth.

This is a most enriching field of study and it cannot be too highly recommended to any who have the resources and opportunity to pursue it. But it soon becomes clear, if you follow this process, that the first of those who believed in the risen Christ had what we would call a 'primitive' understanding of him, and that this progressively grew and filled out. The very earliest strands in the New Testament show that belief in the divinity of Christ grew gradually after Easter. It is quite obvious, when you think of it, that the first disciples of Jesus thought of him as simply a man, like one of them, even if a man specially in touch with, directed by, inspired by, God: a prophet, perhaps *the* latter-day definitive prophet. Then, at and after Easter, they saw him as a man raised by God from the dead; not, as they may have first have thought, brought back to life like Lazarus, but caught up into heaven to share God's own life. Only by degrees did they come to think of Jesus as the Son who shared, indeed shared from the start of his life, the very god-ness of God, his divinity. All of which puts us the question:

Was this growth in understanding of Jesus justified, or was it imagination and loyalty running riot? And how, on what principles, do you answer that question? This book will not try to answer such puzzles by appeal to the inspiration of Scripture: because that raises the question why one believes in the inspiration of Scripture, and leads to a circular position; and because any idea of inspiration one has must be consistent with what can be learned about the texts themselves.

Nor will this book simply appeal to the authority of the teaching Church. Of course, we get our faith within the teaching Church: it fills out and deepens in the course of our life in the Church, and we find it increasingly meaningful and satisfying, and thereby increasingly validated. Is this not enough? Well, it is not enough to satisfy the sharp critic. He will suggest that the Church has buttressed and sustained itself by a tradition established from within by a sort of self-propelling process, which was from the outset founded on unsupported imagination and enthusiasm. So this book will not at the beginning appeal to the authority of the teaching Church, but will, rather, try to show at the end what that authority rests on and why it is justified.

These in outline are the questions and challenges that today's Catholic, or any Christian, has to face. The remaining chapters will try to face them squarely and to show not only that they can be met, and that Christian faith can remain intact, but even that it can deepen and be enriched in the process; to show faith understanding itself better and ending up more sure of its ground. This can be done only by showing what faith in Jesus Christ as risen Lord was based on from the beginning. It might be more heart-warming to write about faith in Jesus Christ in terms of the wonderful richness it gives to life, the force of love that it discovers and releases, the commitment to others that it can engender, the heroisms to which it gives rise, the healing which it brings. But there could well remain some gnawing doubts whether such vivid and real experience of faith can simply justify itself, if it is not in the end based on a true understanding of Jesus. This book aims to ensure that the ground under our feet is firm. The rest can then confidently be built upon it.

2

FAITH

Before we, as it were, roll up our sleeves and tackle the task outlined in the previous chapter, it will be as well to pause and to think briefly about faith in God in general. The reason for doing so is that historical study of texts, however careful and exact, can never by itself account for faith in God; it can never either justify or falsify it. All those who originally followed Jesus, like all those who opposed him, were Jews sharing faith in the God of Israel. Jesus himself was a Jew and shared that faith most profoundly. Their faith in God is already there, already given. All the New Testament can do is to show us what became of Jewish faith in Jesus himself and in his followers. Faith comes first, and the New Testament, when subjected to rigorous study, can show only how that faith developed and expressed itself. So it will be as well to consider briefly some of the qualities of faith in God and to bear these in mind as we consider the New Testament.

Faith in God is not belief *that*: belief that God exists (because there are good reasons for such a conviction), that he is eternal, good, loving, etc. The Jews rightly spoke about 'knowing' God (not knowing about God) and John's Gospel uses this expression a great deal. To believe in God is to be aware of God, in some sense to encounter and recognize him, or to know that one is encountered and addressed by him. Belief in God is not assent to some information about him; it involves some sort of personal meeting. And however much you study the texts of

Judaism or Christianity or any other religion, you cannot just by doing that answer the question, Did they or did they not meet God in the way they said they did? All that texts do is to show how they understood and expressed what they experienced as a meeting with God.

One can put the matter in the more technical terms of theology, 'revelation' and 'faith'. These are correlative terms, i.e. one implies the other. Men can encounter God (have faith), only if God discloses or communicates *himself*. I cannot fall in love with or respond to a person merely by being told all about him or her by someone else. I have to meet and get to know, not just know about, the person. 'Revelation' means that God communicates himself, not just information about himself: he communicates his-self. 'Faith' means that man is aware of, meets, God so communicating his-self: man encounters God in his self-disclosure. If no one 'met God' or got the message when God acted to communicate his-self, then no revelation would take place; God would not in fact have revealed himself. No revelation without faith, and vice versa. Throughout history men in all parts of the world have met God, been aware of God, in life as they found it, in the world of people and things as they experienced it. You can express this, if you wish, by saying that God reveals himself in history; but that is what it means. It is just a fact of human experience. You can share it or be puzzled by it. But you cannot ultimately either justify it or prove it mistaken; any more than you can 'prove' that John and Mary are justified in being in love with each other.

Faith is mysteriously circular. If you are aware of God in your life, you are aware; if you see, you see; if not, not. Argument and discussion can prepare the ground, remove obstacles, improve one's focus, etc, but they cannot either produce faith of themselves or show that it is unjustified. You cannot work your way into faith from the outside simply by vigorous efforts that take the most enlightened means. So faith has been recognized as a gift of God: the Spirit of God himself gives us eyes to see, eyes to recognize him communicating himself to us in human life. Both revelation and faith are God's activity. Faith is self-authenticating, like love, because it basically *is* love, the response of person to person. And it remains mysterious and circular, like love.

Some recent authors who firmly believe in God have argued that there is nothing in the historical evidence provided by the New Testament and in their whole Christian experience that justifies their saying more about Jesus than that he was a good man, in a very full sense inspired by God, a great prophet, a great religious leader like many others in other great religions. Their position must be respected as an honest one, reached after much thought and probably heart searching. But it also needs to be very carefully examined. If they mean that they do not personally encounter God communicating his very self in Jesus Christ in a unique way, well and good. You cannot argue anyone into or out of faith. But if they mean that encountering God in a unique way in Jesus must, and can only, be produced by careful examination of the historical evidence, then what they are implying is both untrue and inconsistent. It is inconsistent because they already believe in God: therefore at some point in their experience of life and their interpretation of it they have gone beyond, and seen beyond, the best that human sciences can tell us about the world and life; so they cannot then say that it cannot be so in the case of Jesus, but only that it is not so for them. It is untrue because God reveals himself and enables men to be aware of and respond to him; men do not discover God.

This book concentrates on Christian faith. But it does not thereby mean to exclude the idea that there is faith in God in other religions and perhaps also in other stances in life that do not look religious at first sight. Indeed if, as seems certain, God gives his grace to all men, then faith must be a constant factor in human experience—greater or lesser faith, more rudimentary or more developed faith, more focused and aware faith or faith more at the edges of awareness. In all his characteristically human experiences of knowing and ever searching to know more, in loving and longing, in his creative arts, in his inexhaustible hope—just as in all his hating and despairing and sorrowing and being blocked and frustrated—in his heights and depths, in his ecstasies and sufferings, man touches on, and is dimly aware that he is touching on, an absolute that both grounds and sustains but also encompasses human life. Much has been written about this pervasive 'horizon' knowledge of God or ability to know God. But it is beyond the scope of this book to explore the question or to examine how Christian faith is related to other faiths in God.

It is necessary to emphasize the element of vision that there is in faith in order, if not to explain, at least to draw attention to its heart and core as a meeting with God, a recognition of God, a response to God discerned through and beyond those confines of human life that can be studied by historians, economists, psychologists, natural scientists etc. But Christian faith grows out of and is a fulfilment, a coming to fullness, of Jewish faith. One of the keynotes of both is a strong reliance on God's faithfulness and promises, a strong element of hope. So Christian faith is both a vision of the present, a vision or awareness of the involvement of Father, Son and Spirit in our present life, and a hope for, a confident longing for, the fullness of the future. This is the characteristic attitude of New Testament writers. They live in a tension between the 'already' and the 'not yet', and we must not over-emphasize either element at the expense of the other. Christ *has* died; Christ *is* risen; Christ *will* come again. Already, for Paul, we are baptized into the death and resurrection of Christ; already his Spirit dwells in us, making us new creatures, sons and daughters by adoption, members of Christ's risen body; we are acceptable to God because of our faith, and do not come under the condemnation that threatens sinners. Already, for John, we are sharers in an eternal life which does not merely begin when this life is over, but is already born in us: the Spirit given to us wells up from inside us into eternal life. But at the same time it is obvious that we are not yet risen, that we are not yet freed from pain and sorrow, not yet free of the drag and temptations of mortal nature; indeed, not only man but the whole of creation suffers the birth-pangs of the Kingdom. Christ has conquered all the forces that assail man in the world, and has claimed the world as a kingdom for his Father: but the world, not yet subject to him, has not yet entered fully into his victory. So the vision opens out into a new hope, a new longing, a confident expectation of God's faithfulness to the new covenant and promise he has established in the death and resurrection of Christ.

Finally, as we know only too well, faith is obscure. And this we can partly understand just from the fact that faith is compounded with hope: it is a hope-vision; it is not a clear vision, but a hazy one. Paul, thinking of the reflection you might see in a polished metal mirror, said 'in a glass, darkly'. It is not an absolutely rock-like expectation, but a hope that is sometimes shaky. This is not because God sets out deliberately, as it were, to test and try us. It is because the Spirit already dwelling (Paul) or abiding (John) in us does not yet totally possess and has not yet totally transformed us. So we are subject to the ups and downs of any human experience. We ought to get a clue and an encouragement about this from the well-documented experience of mystical prayer. It would be wrong to imagine that 'the mystics' are so much in a class apart, so much the recipients of God's special graces, that we run-of-the-mill Christians have nothing to learn from them, or that there is no continuity between our faith and prayer and theirs. On the contrary, their faith-life, just because it is in some sense more advanced, should be able to throw a lot of light on ours. Much has been written on this topic. Here it must suffice to recall two things, and bear them in mind as we turn to consider the faith of the first Christians.

The first thing is that faith can be said to have two components. There is the outside world, human life in the world, in which God communicates himself. And there are the 'eyes to see', the inside world of our awareness: and God communicates himself there, too. We are aware of his Spirit dwelling, giving life, giving vision and love within us. We may feel rather uncertain about asserting this with confidence, and it is here that mystical experience helps. For in mystical experience it is the inner revelation that develops: the mystic becomes increasingly aware of God 'dwelling', being in possession, not as an object but as a source of one's own being, at the centre of the soul. That clarifies what may seem somewhat thin, or hazy, or dissipated, in our own faith and prayer: when we read about it we recognize its germ in ourselves.

The second thing to learn from the mystics is that the obscurity of faith enters in their case into a deeper form of darkness. The heart has to go out beyond where the mind, where ordinary vision and understanding, can take one. There has to be, already, a deep knowledge and love of God as a person addressing me and calling for my response. But at the point or gateway, if one may so speak, of mystical prayer it is love that has to develop on its own, to take the lead out into the darkness. And then (when it is possible to speak only in paradox) the darkness itself becomes a new sort of light and a new vision of the heart develops. But how, we may ask, does this clarify our own more ordinary faith and prayer? It is hard to find a wholly satisfactory form of words for the answer, so a very simple one is offered: it is part of the mystery of faith that only he who loves can truly see it.

3

THE NEW TESTAMENT

This chapter will try to fill out a bit the outline given in the first chapter of the kind of problem that arises for the Christian believer out of today's serious study of the New Testament. We need to see the shape of the problem, the shape of the question posed, with sufficient clarity in order to be able to see what the answer to it might be.

Study of Matthew, Mark and Luke shows that they are the end-product of between thirty and sixty years of reflection and experience of Christian living. It is doubtful to what extent any of these books has 'an author' in the modern sense: the authors could very well be whole Christian communities in different places, working over verbal material they had earlier received, or continued to receive, from other communities. The material has been organized in fairly clear patterns and sections: for purposes of teaching and preaching; for use in worship; to make it easier to remember. Each Gospel has its own 'theology' or special set of insights that it wants to put over. For instance, Luke intends to bring out the action of the Holy Spirit in Jesus' origins and the whole of his life; the importance of women in the story is emphasized; there is concentration on the poor; there is some attempt to present Christianity as a moderate and reasonable sort of religion to the Roman authorities; Jesus' prediction of the imminent coming of the Son of Man, as narrated by Mark, is soft-pedalled and Christians are encouraged to accept the idea of living their faith in the world. Matthew and Mark have other and different aims. Most people think Mark is the earliest Gospel, but it is already a growth from earlier material. Gospels grew in communities, and stories have grown in the telling. Not only do different versions of Jesus' sayings occur, but sometimes sayings occur in different contexts which alter their meanings, and so one is left in doubt about the original saying and its exact point. Conversely, we sometimes find the same scene in two Gospels, but as settings for different sayings of Jesus. The possible interactions of the growing processes on one another present a puzzle of great complexity, to which nobody has offered a solution satisfactory to everyone else.

One fairly simple example of differences is the Our Father. It is not in Mark. The version we are used to is in Matthew. Luke simply has, 'Father (may thy name be blessed), thy kingdom come. Give us each day our bread for the day; and forgive us our sins, for we too forgive all who have wronged us. And do not bring us to the test.' In Luke the disciples asked Jesus, 'Lord, teach us to pray,' after they had seen him at prayer. In Matthew it is perhaps less an instruction about what prayers to make, because Jesus introduces it in the long gathering together of his teaching we call the Sermon on the Mount with the words, 'When you pray, don't babble on like the pagans . . . your Father knows all your needs before you ask him.' The point, then, seems to be not so much the content of the prayer but its brevity and simplicity. And yet, paradoxically, it would appear that in Matthew's Church additions in the form of parallel clauses interpreting the previous clause have been made, e.g. 'Thy kingdom come, (which means) thy will be done on earth as it is in heaven.'

There are eight (or nine) 'beatitudes' in Matthew, while Luke has four beatitudes and four corresponding woes, which is typical of his stylistic arrangement. Matthew's blessings are more spiritualized than those of Luke, who speaks of the poor, the hungry, the weeping. There are three predictions of the

Passion in each of these three Gospels: in the second Luke has no reference to the resurrection; in the third Matthew has Jesus saying not merely that they will kill him, but specifically that they will crucify him. Commentators think that, whereas Jesus would have seen that the mounting opposition against him would lead to his death, the details of his Passion and the fact of resurrection may well have been written in afterwards: how otherwise can the disciples simply 'not have understood'; and if Jesus had foretold it all so clearly, how could it all have been so unexpected?

Far more complex examples are the titles 'Son of Man' and 'Messiah' (Christ). After Easter, believing Christians certainly hailed the Risen One by these titles, but later usage has to a greater or lesser extent been read back into the sayings of Jesus. Close study of the matter makes it pretty certain that Jesus did not accept the title Messiah which others fastened on to him, because it gave the wrong idea of his mission from the Father. It is uncertain whether he used the phrase 'Son of Man', except perhaps in the senses of 'man' and 'I'; but whether sayings about the Son of Man coming on the clouds of heaven refer to himself, and precisely what meanings should be given to it in different cases, remain a great puzzle.

These few examples may not seem to add up to much. But when the examples become hundreds, when every verse of the Gospels has been minutely examined in the light of Old Testament parallels, other literature of the time and other Gospels, and in the light of various adaptations to situations in which Christian communities later found themselves, one is left with the conviction that we are at some remove from the actual words and deeds of Jesus in their original context. Christians have long prayed and thought over what Jesus said and did, and have entered into a deeper understanding, especially seeing him as a coming to fulfilment of familiar aspirations, themes and passages in the Old Testament. And it becomes clear that, while we have first-hand evidence of the life and thinking of the believing Church, and find new riches in the writings for that very reason, we do not have a record of how Jesus was seen, heard and understood at the time. To what extent such a record can be recovered from the Gospels as they stand is a matter of widely diverging opinions.

The Infancy Narratives in Matthew and Luke raise a different kind of question. They differ from each other in almost every way, Joseph being the centre of Matthew's narrative and Mary of Luke's: but the virgin birth is common to both. If John and Paul knew this material, it is very odd indeed that they never refer to it, particularly in certain places. Matthew's genealogy is quite different from Luke's, and can hardly be meant to be taken literally; it is a stylistic arrangement in three cycles of 2 x 7 generations, corresponding to the three main periods of Israel's history, to show that Jesus brings to fulfilment the history of Israel and its heroes. Luke's whole infancy story is arranged in a complex literary pattern, like those old hinged paintings called diptychs ('twofolds'): parallel annunciations and births, of John the Baptist and Jesus, with parallel canticles of Zacchary and Mary, the Magnificat being a reshaping of Anna's canticle in the First Book of Samuel. All this raises the question as to whether the evangelists themselves meant the narratives to be understood as historical records rather than symbolic stories, drawing heavily on Old Testament material, intended to bring out the heavenly origin of Jesus.

John's Gospel is one of the greatest pieces of literature of all time. The evangelist is like an organist with three or four hands, playing simultaneously on different registers. A characteristic pattern is the three-tier one: Jesus' saying is rather stupidly taken literally by the person he is speaking to (e.g. Nicodemus and the saying about being 'born again', as the word could also mean 'from above'), so that the Christian reader can smile to himself; there is the true spiritual meaning which Jesus intended; and there is the meaning for John's community living in resurrection faith. There is so much going on all the time in the very simply told story. Chapter 9, for instance, about the man born blind, is 'really' about the gentiles who were born outside God's revelation to Israel, but came to 'see', to have the eyes of Christian faith (like John's Church); and the Jews who were born 'seeing' but became blind. Again, the gospel begins with 'In the beginning', like the Book of Genesis, and the early chapters are thought to have been arranged as the seven days of the New Creation, to parallel the seven days of the first creation. However, the more one marvels at the artistry and subtle blendings of spiritual message, the more one realizes that one is not reading a record of what was said and of how it was understood at the time. The fourth Gospel is a sublime Christian meditation, artistically arranged. It has its own literary pattern of narrative followed by long discourses which bring out the fullest meaning of Jesus' actions and miracles: the miracles are all signs of who he is for those who have eyes to see. The Jesus of John is a far more divine figure throughout than the Jesus of Matthew, Mark and Luke: he is the Word (or Wisdom) of God become frail man like us ('flesh'), and no one thought of him like that in his lifetime. One can be sure that many original sources and bits of material are embedded in John, whose stories of Jesus are mostly peculiar to himself, but there is no way of constructing the original scene; yet, at the same time, something of the simplicity and excitement of first-hand experience and reporting shines through the very artistry of the arrangement. However as we have them, the long discourses of Jesus are Christian meditations, different versions sometimes appearing side by side. And the narratives are 'staged': in the story of the Samaritan woman in Chapter 4, there are successive dialogues about the living water, true worship of the Father, true food and the harvest, with Jesus and the person to whom he is talking alternating in opening the dialogue; the trial scene is arranged in seven episodes, alternating inside and outside, with catchwords denoting entrances and exits.

So the Gospels as they stand are a record of Christian faith in Jesus, seeing him anew in the light of Easter and of Pentecost, and of the prayer and life of the early Church. They show developing ideas of God's purposes in Jesus and a growing sense of his divinity. The question they put to us is: Are we to take all this as a truer and deeper view of Jesus, guided by the Holy Spirit, or are we to regard it as an unchecked growth of religious devotion? And, in any case, what can we really know about what Jesus thought and said and did, and about how people reacted to him at the time?

Acts of Apostles (as is its Greek name, meaning some deeds of some apostles) is generally agreed to be by Luke and to date towards the end of whatever period you allow for the development of New Testament writing. It continues the theological themes of Luke's Gospel: for instance, just as the Spirit brought about the birth and growing to maturity of Jesus, so the Spirit brings the Church to birth and growth. Acts has a number of set speeches, just like the writings of classic Greek historians, notably Thucydides: the author composes polished speeches expressing what was appropriate to the occasion, and no doubt containing original material. Very significant are the shorter and longer addresses in which Peter and Paul proclaim the essential Christian Gospel. Scholars argue about the extent to which later ideas have been read back into earlier occasions, about what elements are 'primitive' and what are due to later theologies as formulated by Luke; but on the whole one can get a fair picture of the very simple ideas of judgement and forgiveness in which the risen Jesus was first proclaimed, and observe the filling out of the proclamation by later theologies. Acts presents many puzzles. The author regards Paul as his hero, and yet reflects hardly at all the questions and answers which actually preoccupied Paul, as we know from his letters. Acts gives three accounts of Paul's conversion: they are not consistent with one another in details, and are very unlike the little that Paul says about it himself. One has to give priority to first-hand over second-hand evidence. There are good reasons for thinking that the account of 'the Council of Jerusalem' (as we have come to call it) in Acts Chapter 15 is a running together of two separate occasions, in the first of which Peter was the leading figure, and in the second James: the first dealt with the question of fundamental importance, whether Christians should be circumcized and obey the Jewish Law, remaining as part of Judaism, or whether that was now superseded; the second occasion dealt with a few legal and practical consequences of the first decision. What is extremely puzzling is that we know from Paul's letters that he was greatly exercised by precisely these questions; that Acts represents him as being present at 'the Council' and being sent with Barnabas and others to convey its decisions to the Church at Antioch; yet that nowhere in his letters, when arguing and giving answers about these questions, does Paul make any reference to their having been authoritatively decided in this way.

These are some notable puzzles that arise from studying Acts as one of a set of historical texts. Not only do they make it difficult to decide how reliable is Luke's account of the origins and early years of the Church, but they also pose the same question that arises from the Gospels: is the growth from a more primitive to a more developed theology of Jesus a God-guided development or a matter of human embroidering and enthusiasm?

If the preceding paragraphs fairly represent the shape of the problem we are trying to tackle, then, before proceeding to look for an answer in the texts themselves, it may be as well for us to stand back and make one or two general observations in order to get the perspective right.

The first thing to remark is that it is *the Gospels precisely as we have them* that have fashioned Christian history over the centuries and have exercised such enormous power over millions of ordinary and extraordinary Christian lives, and not

some more accurate historical record of what the historical Jesus thought, said and did, which we might today wish to distil from them. From this obvious remark one or two things follow and we need to be as clear headed as possible about them.

One thing that follows can best be put as a negative, leaving other possibilities open for further investigation. It is that our Christian faith today does not rest solely on, is not justified solely by, the life and death of Jesus. It does not follow that it rests solely on the New Testament as a record of early Christian faith in which Jesus is seen through the filter of resurrection faith. Many would wish to argue that, nevertheless, this is the case. They would say, and it would be absurd and impossible to deny, that the New Testament is a book of immense spiritual power, that generations have been nourished by it, that we still experience its force today as we confront today's world, today's problems, today's puzzles about the meaning of life. They would say that God speaks to us through it. All can agree on that. But they would go on to say that this is sufficient; that for them the New Testament validates itself as God's word, and not of merely human devising; and that therefore this record of early Christian faith is a fully adequate and sufficient basis and justification for Christian faith today. This would be their answer to the question we have faced, their ground of certainty that the post-Easter growth in understanding of Jesus was the work of God's Spirit and not a matter of unwarranted human elaboration. However, the following chapters will argue that, though this is a great part of the answer, something more is needed. Certainly, part of what goes to the making of Christian faith today is the ability to recognize the authority and power of God at work in Jesus just as our Gospels present him. But one would hesitate to say that the New Testament attests solely the action of God's Spirit, because the history of the Church always also reflects the inadequacy and sometimes feebleness of man's response to God. And if faith consists in encountering God, how satisfactory is it to say that I meet and respond to the person, God, in prayerful reflection on even the greatest written witness to his works or that I meet and respond to the risen Jesus himself in meditating the record of faith in him?

Another thing that follows from recognizing that it has been the Gospels and other New Testament writings precisely as we have them which have been such a great religious force over the centuries, is of very considerable importance. It is, quite simply, that the less you attribute to Jesus and to the action of God's Spirit among the early Christians, the more you must necessarily attribute to the inventive religious genius of the first followers of Jesus and of those who came after them. If it is historical evidence that biblical scholars (quite rightly in their field of work) insist on, then let us look at the historical evidence. There is nothing in it to suggest that the followers of Jesus were that sort of religious genius, holy and good men though they were. It is not just a matter of what this man or that might have contributed to such a powerful religious force; it is the cohesiveness of the whole.

It is an absorbing exercise to try to lay out on a time-line the gradual development of Christian theologies in the early Church. But however far you can push back towards the primitive understanding of Jesus, there is already a pretty sophisticated theological method at work: Jesus is ever more deeply comprehended 'according to the scriptures', meaning of course the Old Testament; he is ever more fully seen as the coming to fullness of all the aspirations of Israel, all the great themes of Jewish theology, and that not in just a general sort of way but with profound and careful reflection on many particular texts in Israel's heritage. Ah, but what about Paul: he surely was a religious genius? Yes, he certainly was. He had also been educated in the scholarship of the time, and so had the tools of expression which Galilean fishermen lacked. Some biblical experts of former times have written as if Paul had invented Christianity, or at any rate Catholicism. Nobody today would take such a view. Paul did not invent Christianity, he joined it.

And it is precisely Paul who is witness to the fact that, when he first proclaimed the Gospel in Corinth about 50 AD, he 'handed on to you the facts that had been imparted to me: that Christ died for our sins, in accordance with the scriptures . . .' (I Cor. 15:3). The theological method is already there; it must have been imparted to him soon after his conversion about 35 AD.

This general sort of consideration, which could simply be termed common sense, sets limits to 'radical' views of the New Testament. It would be idiotic, in the name of scholarly doubts, to search for religious genius everywhere except in Jesus.

Which brings us to the last general consideration. It is the matter of the wood and the trees, the matter of the real Jesus in danger of being lost amid the trees, branches and indeed twigs, of scholarship. This is a grievance that anyone getting down to the details of New Testament study is liable to feel (the most over-researched book in history, someone said), a danger of which anyone dealing with great literature is bound to be aware. The distinguishing feature by which the historical Jesus can be recognized in all the stories and sayings, whatever the accretions and overlaid interpretations, is his sovereign assurance of speaking for his Father, the immediacy and directness of his message, the way in which in his teaching, his parables and his deeds, he made people vividly aware of the presence of God's saving power. He did not merely tell them about it; he made it real, tangible to them. He embodied it. His teaching, his answers, his parables, broke through all assumptions with the force of something new, however many phrases and images of his can be found in other contemporary sources: after all, he could only use available language. His miracles conveyed the same immediate, caring, saving power of God. Yes, they may have been embroidered and added to in the telling. But if he did not work any, why was he accused of working them by the power of Beelzebub? That bears the stamp of historical accuracy: Christian apologetic would not have invented it. The mystery or compelling force of Jesus was to make the reality of God, his kingdom and his will, present. The Gospels call this his 'authority' in word and deed: it is a pet word in Matthew. It carries the overtones of faith in who he is, a faith probably never explicit in anyone at the time; but it also conveys unmistakably his contemporary impact, which drew crowds to him and bound to him lifelong followers. The genius was unquestionably his.

The way forward at this point is important. It would be wholly unsatisfactory to feel that you *had* to be 'conservative' about biblical scholarship in order to be secure in your Christian faith; that you had to fend off unwelcome conclusions about Scripture, however reasonably and intelligently argued; that you had your back to some sort of wall and could only hold on to faith by to some extent closing your eyes and your mind. What would be satisfactory would be to be able to see that it does not very much matter, within defensible limits, whether you are at the conservative or radical end of the scale, because the security or ground or justification of Christian faith does not depend on that but is to be found elsewhere. The ensuing chapters will offer a way to that position. In the course of doing so they will at points be prepared to take a more or less radical view of some central issues, not because that is necessarily the more correct or more intelligent or more generally approved view, but just to show that it does not affect the heart of the matter; to show that the ground under our feet is not precisely there.

4

THE RESURRECTION

Believing Christians are liable to get very uptight and to react violently if you start discussing whether the resurrection was a historical event. So one is inclined to begin with a plea for coolness and for a readiness to 'hear' what is being said, even when it is difficult to find the right words for it. To suggest that the resurrection itself, as opposed to its effects in history, is not to be thought of as a historical event, is not to suggest that it is not true, that it did not happen. To urge that the resurrection is not properly thought of as a historical event is not to undervalue it or to say that it is less than a historical event: on the contrary, it is to urge that it is a great deal more and that, if anyone insists on calling it a historical event, they may themselves be undervaluing it and to some extent closing their minds and hearts to what is central about it.

Let us start with some negatives. No one witnessed the 'event' of the resurrection: there were witnesses only to some historical events associated with it, to what human beings saw and heard. This is not the same as saying no one saw the risen Christ: it is only saying that no one saw him, as it were, rising. Secondly, resurrection is not resuscitation: Jesus did not return from the grave to our form of life, like Lazarus, to die again another day.

The negatives point to the positive. To confess the resurrection is to confess that Jesus, the whole man, entered into eternal life, entered into sharing the life of God. It is perfectly natural and proper that we should have pictorial words and images about the resurrection: what other words have we? 'Resurrection' suggests that a body, lying prostrate in death, sat up, stood up, and began to live again as a person: like Lazarus or the little girl Jesus brought back to (this) life. There would be historical evidence for or against such a bringing back to life. Jesus' acts of raising people from the dead were signs of the greater reality of his own resurrection: they were not previous resurrections. What is central to the resurrection of Christ is his risen-ness, his sharing in the life of God permanently, invincibly, indestructibly. And that is not something that goes on in history, goes on within the confines of this mortal life, so that we can subject it to our normal scrutinies so as to be sure about it; or, indeed, so as to disprove it.

John tries to convince us that we are here and now born again into a totally new and other sort of life than the one we can scrutinize by our sciences: Father, Son and Spirit come to abide in us; the life of the Trinity is lived in us. It was Nicodemus who foolishly took 'being born again' literally. Paul goes very far out in insisting that the risen Christ does not live the soul-life we now live, but spirit-life: 'the last Adam has become a life-giving Spirit' (I Cor. 15:45). He does not of course mean that he has ceased to be a man: it is the resurrection of Jesus that he is talking about, and his whole argument depends on Jesus' risen humanity's somehow gathering our humanity into his sharing of the life of God. But he does want to prevent the Corinthians from having 'earthy' or too physical ideas of the resurrection.

The resurrection is therefore undervalued, or even wholly misunderstood, if it is thought of as simply a historical event: because that is a failure to grasp the deep mystery of historical man's being transposed into a divine key and really sharing the eternal life of God; and because, if it is simply a historical event, then it can be proved or disproved by historians, by the best scholarship of the human sciences, including that of biblical

scholars. And our faith does not ultimately rest on what historical or any other scholars can prove. It rests on our encountering God in our own experience of life. There could, of course, be historical evidence for the empty tomb. And a vision or seeing of the risen Christ would be a historical event, an experience had by a person in history: for him the risen Christ would have intersected history. But the risen Christ himself *is* not in history: his existence is heavenly, at the end or bounds of history, eschatological; and his heavenly and risen existence can affect all history, not only that subsequent to his life and death; he can give his grace to all men.

The upshot is that the resurrection, i.e. Christ in his risenness, is and can only be an object of faith. There can be many historical events leading to, pointing to, substantiating the resurrection, but these cannot conclude to it. The risen Christ can manifest himself to men, but they can grasp him in his manifestation only with the eyes, the vision, of faith, and not as a this-worldly being.

When we turn to the gospel accounts of Jesus' appearances to his disciples after his death, we find that they are not consistent with one another, even as to whether Jesus appeared to them in Jerusalem or in Galilee. The whole ground has been gone over in a number of books. Merely to try to 'harmonize' the accounts, to fit them together into one complete story, is to ignore the fact that we have traditions that are simply different and at many points unknown to one another; and the possibility or probability of any of the accounts' having grown in the course of time. It is possible to tell in general which are the earlier and which the later narratives, and it is noticeable that the later are the more elaborate. Luke in particular stresses the physical aspect of Jesus' appearances. It is considerations such as these which have led some critics to the conviction that faith in the resurrection came first, and produced both the appearance stories and the empty tomb stories; that the appearances and the empty tomb did not produce resurrection faith, but *vice versa*. These critics then have to try to understand how resurrection faith originated.

Now this is a very crucial and sensitive point for understanding Christian faith. We might well think that the balance of argument goes against taking such a radical position. But at the same time we are conscious that we need to ground our faith on what we are certain about, and not merely on what is probable or even highly probable. So this is precisely the point at which to try to discern what seems fundamental and necessary for Christian faith, to focus and isolate it in such a way that thereafter there is freedom to take a more radical or more conservative view of resurrection narratives, without this affecting the central issue. So, simply for the sake of argument, let us discount the empty tomb and the appearance stories and see if there is not something more fundamental.

First the empty tomb, not mentioned by Paul, which does not, of course, prove that he did not know about it: he just does not list it among the basic elements of the Gospel which he later reminds the Corinthians that he handed over to them (I Cor. 15:3). In saying that Jesus died, was buried, and rose again on the third day, he may mean to imply that Jesus left his tomb. The empty tomb did not play a part for him or for the Corinthians in their coming to faith. However, if we are clear that the resurrection of Jesus is a matter of faith, that the risen Jesus is an object of faith, then it is certainly possible to believe that the Father gathered him into eternal life even if his body never left the tomb; possible to say that the empty tomb is not essential to faith in the resurrection, that the mystery and truth of the resurrection do not stand or fall with the empty tomb. In the same way it is possible to believe that we in our turn enter (the fullness of) eternal life immediately at death, though our bodies lie in the grave. Resurrection is such a mystery anyway, that we are misguided in trying to think out how God gathers and sorts out all the material particles, or to try to confine God's action within any other mechanism of our own understanding. As has been said above, Paul, in trying to convey the idea of resurrection to the Corinthians, stresses the difference between the earthly self and the heavenly self, the physical or natural and the spiritual: 'I tell you this, brethren: flesh and blood cannot inherit the kingdom of God, nor does the perishable inherit the imperishable' (I Cor. 15:50). Yet it is resurrected human beings and not just 'souls' that he is talking about.

At the same time, however true it is that more sophisticated thinking can encompass the idea of Jesus' rising from the dead without his dead body's leaving the tomb, it is in the highest degree improbable that anyone at the time would have believed the proclamation of the first witnesses that Jesus had risen and had appeared to them, if in fact this had not been coupled with clear evidence of an empty tomb.

If, however, as the more radical critics argue, faith in the resurrection came before (and accounted for) the appearance stories and the empty tomb stories, then how did it come? It is surely not right to suppose that belief in the resurrection arose out of a rallying of courage and conviction among some disciples (grouped round Peter?), a resurgence of faith in Jesus that came to them after the devastating events of the Passion, a second wind of confidence as they looked back on the enormous impact Jesus had made on them, and the fact that he had already mediated salvation to them in his lifetime—all building up to the conviction that Jesus was too great to die: he must be alive. What God wrought in Jesus must go on, etc. Even if one wishes to argue that God inspired such a confidence in them and in that way revealed the resurrection of Jesus to them (thereby accepting the fact of the resurrection), it is surely against common sense to suppose that such a conviction could have been so firm in them, could have been caught with such enthusiasm by others, could have led so rapidly to the birth and growth of the Church, if there had been simply nothing whatever to assert or point to apart from the life and death of

Jesus and their own inner conviction. Furthermore, it is flat against the evidence. All the evidence points to complete dejection and loss of hope among the disciples: there is no evidence at all for a rallying of faith and courage coming from inside of them. No: the evidence is that something happened *to* the first witnesses, which was of a sudden and totally unexpected nature, and not a product of their own rallying enthusiasm. Something later happened to Paul, equally out of the blue.

It is at this point important to distinguish appearances of Jesus from appearance stories. Even if the stories developed later as ways of elaborating what was meant by 'appearance' and what was meant by resurrection, there remains at their base the same structure of an event in which quite unexpectedly Jesus appeared to his followers; they did not work it up, it happened to them. Gospels as they stand are later texts than Paul's letters, though on any reckoning they must have many elements going back before Paul to Easter and to Jesus' life. Paul openly claims: 'Am I not an apostle? Have I not seen (or, Did I not see) the Lord?' (I Cor. 9:1). There is the basic claim, 'I have seen the Lord,' which is one hallmark of the chosen apostle (the other being that in his appearings Jesus commissioned the witnesses to preach the Gospel). Paul has no appearance stories, in the sense of scenes in which Jesus appears and talks to his followers in different settings, which is not to say that he did not know the stories. But his own faith and his own apostleship are based on the experience covered by that lapidary phrase: 'I have seen the Lord.' It turns up again, in what may well be the other end of the New Testament, in John's account of the appearance to Mary Magdalen, after which she rushes off to tell the disciples, 'I have seen the Lord' (John 20:18); and again when, in the next story, the apostles who had witnessed Jesus' Easter-day appearance tell Thomas, 'We have seen the Lord' (John 20:25). The kindly Barnabas introduced Paul to the hesitant apostles in Jerusalem, and Paul 'recounted to them how he had seen the Lord on his journey, and that he had talked to him' (Acts 9:27). In his brief reminder to the Corinthians of what he had first preached to them, Paul uses the same simple word: 'he was seen by Cephas, then the twelve; then he was seen by more than five hundred brethren . . . then he was seen by James, then by all the apostles: last of all he was seen by me . . .' (I Cor. 15:5–8). Rivers of scholarly ink have been poured out to show that in this passive form ('was seen by') the use of this simplest of Greek words, and commonest of Greek constructions, mean something unusual and sophisticated by way of an interior spiritual vision, or conviction engendered by God, of Jesus' risen-ness. The arguments seem to ignore the fact that Paul's use of 'I have seen the Lord' shows the equivalence of the active and passive forms—for him. And how could the Corinthians be expected to understand some such refined meaning as 'God made known interiorly' from such straightforward language? Acts 26:16 also shows the equivalence of the active and passive expressions, when in his third account of Paul's conversion Luke writes: 'I am Jesus whom you are persecuting. But arise and stand on your own two feet. The reason why I was seen by you was to appoint you my servant and witness both to what you have seen of me and what you will yet see.' Surely we can recognize in this recurrent phrase in very different New Testament texts the primitive apostolic witness, 'I have seen the Lord.' A later chapter will tease out what in this expression is meant by 'the Lord'. But the evidence seems irresistible that 'I have seen', quite independently of scene-setting stories, is where it all started. And it conveys something equivalent to objective seeing, and not an interior conviction.

It was necessary for the first witnesses of the resurrection, as it is right and proper for us, to use simple pictorial language to express their message. Pictorial language will express a mystery beyond our grasp very well, as long as we remind ourselves that we are using pictures as symbols of heavenly reality, and are not tied fast to our own pictures. 'Resurrection' (the rising up of a dead body, as if from sleep), 'ascension' (the bodily person going up into the sky), and 'elevation' (God the Father lifting Jesus up to his right hand in heaven), are such pictures. The three words are best understood as different pictorial ways of bringing out the one reality of the risen-ness of Christ. Luke alone has an interim period of forty days, after resurrection and before ascension, during which the risen Jesus appears to his disciples. Mark has no appearances, if we accept with nearly all specialists in the field that his Gospel ended at 16:8 and that the remaining verses are later additions modelled on the other Gospels: the evidence is in the manuscripts themselves. Matthew has no reference to ascension. John has Jesus telling Mary Magdalen, 'I have not yet ascended to the Father,' but his own expression is 'glorification' and Jesus is already glorified in his appearances, i.e. sharing the new life with God. It is hard to think of resurrection and ascension or elevation or glorification as separate events, and Luke's interval is best understood as his scheme for setting out in narrative form different factors that are involved in the whole idea of, and belief in, resurrection, viz. the 'whole' Jesus sharing God's life, which is spirit-life and not flesh-life (to use Paul's language), and sending God's Spirit on his followers to form the Church. Luke's scheme separates in time, to assist our imagination, resurrection, ascension and the sending of the Spirit (Pentecost); but the events are in themselves heavenly events, not measurable or separable by time. In John, Jesus gives the Spirit at his first appearance to his assembled disciples (20:22), if not (as some think) in his very act of dying, where John uses the unusual phrase, 'he handed over the spirit' (19:30). Paul recounts appearances, but has no appearance stories or narratives: he is not, of course, writing a gospel. He concentrates on the idea that the risen, ascended and elevated Lord gives the Spirit to his followers to form and gather them into his risen body (self), or perhaps we should say into an extension of his risen body-self, the Church.

It has been argued that the resurrection, in its inner and proper reality as opposed to its effects here on earth, is and can only be an object of faith. In the second chapter we reflected that faith is an obscure sort of seeing in which love goes out beyond where reasoning and evidence can take you, and finds God. We also considered how faith is mysteriously circular: God gives himself and the eyes to recognize him, the heart to know him. One cannot ultimately say why one person believes and another does not: if we could say why, we could reduce it to our own activities, whereas revelation is God's activity. Now it is time to try to put these factors together.

If we take up again the question why it was that Jesus appeared only to his followers and not to people like Caiaphas, the obvious answer may well be the correct one—that he chose to. He appeared to them to commission them as his apostles, to found a community of faith in the Father's self-gift through him, and to preach that faith to the whole world: and only his followers *knew* him, his life and teaching, and were able to 'know' and to proclaim the living Jesus and the risen Christ as one person and one revelation of God. Only they could truly know Jesus as risen. Only they could found the Church. The fact that he appeared later to the hostile Paul suggests that he 'could have' appeared to Caiaphas. There are some complicating factors in the case of Paul, who tells us very little about the appearance to him (I Cor. 9:1; 15:8; Gal. 1:15–16) by contrast with the dramatic but not wholly consistent scenes in Acts, which are to some extent modelled on Old Testament stories. But Paul himself certainly claimed that his seeing of the Lord was the last (implying that there were to be no more) of a series of seeings of the Lord which was unique. However, Paul was not a witness to the living Jesus and did not found the Church; nor, it seems safe to say, could he have done. Appearances at Easter to the hostile would in a true sense have been meaningless. But there is something more to say, which no words can quite capture, because it is about the mystery of resurrection and of faith. If it is true that resurrection is and can only be the object of faith; if God must give 'eyes to see' in order that the Lord, the known Jesus as risen, should be 'seen'; then in some sense that eludes our final grasp: only those who loved could see. Church-founding appearances could be only to the devoted followers. This is not to say that their love of Jesus produced their seeing, for the action is God's. In order to understand the matter a little more fully (as long as we realize that we shall not understand it wholly), we should reflect that the division between those who believed and those who did not does not begin at Easter. It starts right back in the life of Jesus, between those who became aware of the 'authority', the power and presence, of God at work in him—in his actions, teachings, parables, in his life-style, in a word in *him*—and those who did not. His disciples became progressively aware of this. If we accept the attractive explanation of Mark's Gospel as an attempt from within the believing Church to show 'what it was like at the time', the disciples did not get very far. This Gospel makes them out as pretty dim (from the later vantage point of Easter faith), and is purposely structured around episodes which bring out Jesus' exasperation with their slowness to see, understand, believe. At the end of the last of these blocks of narrative, Jesus points up the message by curing a blind man! But they did love, even if they did not see very much. It has been urged above that it is clean contrary to the evidence to argue from their pre-crucifixion love and dawning faith that these alone sufficed to bring them a post-crucifixion conviction that Jesus was risen. Their faith was not all that developed, and Calvary prostrated it. Only Jesus himself could revive it. This he did in appearing to them, which he could do (we have to use what categories of thought we can) because, though their faith and hope had virtually gone, their love remained.

'Yet some doubted' (Matt. 28:17): on the face of it, this surprising remark is made of some of the eleven to whom Jesus appeared on the appointed mountain in Galilee. Most if not all of the appearance stories reflect this element of uncertainty among the disciples: Mary Magdalen, Thomas, the disciples on the road to Emmaus and at the lakeside, are notable examples. It has the ring of historicity: would a carefully planned apologetic or worked-up enthusiasm have included this? The risen Jesus is hard to recognize, in the garden of his tomb or by the lakeside *even* by his most devoted followers. Faith is not only mysteriously circular but, as we know only too well, it is obscure, a dark vision. But the resurrection faith of the leading apostles was deep, unshakable, passionate, and became a world force. How or why? Because they had seen the Lord. But also because of that second key factor, which we must next consider, and which throws further light on the question we have just been considering.

To summarize, then, before proceeding: Biblical scholars may adduce reasons for doubting the authenticity of the appearance stories. But neither historical nor scientific learning can either prove or disprove whether Jesus in his risen-ness appeared to, was seen by, the first chosen witnesses: it simply lies outside the scope of human sciences. We have argued that the great weight of evidence is that the first chosen witnesses were convinced they *had* 'seen the Lord' in a unique way, not available to others; and that they did not mean by this just some intense interior illumination, which others could share, but something corresponding for them to objective vision.

5

THEIR FAITH

The other key factor, or perhaps the other half of the same key factor, is the outpouring of the Spirit. It will be as well to approach this subject with another question in mind: why did others believe in the resurrection, who had not themselves 'seen the Lord'? This approach should lead us to understand more fully the faith of the earliest Christians and what it was grounded on.

It has already been observed that Luke's timetable of forty days from Easter to the Ascension, and then the experience of the Spirit on the day of Pentecost ten days later (Pentecost means the fiftieth day after the Passover), looks like a formal scheme or arrangement: indeed, a scheme based on Jewish feasts—the Feast of Unleavened Bread and the Feast of First Fruits, with the traditional number forty chosen for the ascension. Luke, we reflected, was spreading out in time as separate events, essential 'moments' in the one reality of resurrection-ascension-elevation, to assist the understanding of his readers. If it is correct to consider the early chapters of Acts in this way, then it provides us with an important clue.

The fact that there is no other account against which to check the accuracy of Acts about the early beginnings of the Church, and the doubts about accuracy that the book itself raises at various points, make some scholars very doubtful how much the narrative of Acts can be relied on. For our purposes it does not matter what position is taken on this question: when there is no other evidence, a historian must follow at least the broad lines of the only available evidence, at risk of making up his own version for which there is no evidence at all. And there is corroboration for these broad lines from the first-hand evidence of Paul. The account of Pentecost in Acts may be the concentration in a single event of what was characteristic in the beginnings of the Church in successive times and places; it may also preserve the tradition of a notably powerful original experience shared by quite a large group comprising others besides those who claimed to have seen the Lord.

Acts 1:15 speaks of a company of 120; and Acts 2:1 simply follows on with, 'When the day of Pentecost had come, they were all together in one place.' The point is that in either case vivid experience of the Spirit is a basic and pervasive characteristic of the early Church. It is this that Paul corroborates: *experience* of the Spirit, not thinking or talking about the Spirit. Just as the appearance narratives have the basic structure of something unexpected happening to the witnesses, so Acts and Paul are talking about people being acted upon, not people working themselves up.

Nearly all the appearance stories have in one way or another the character of Jesus commissioning his followers to go out and proclaim his resurrection. They are not appearances to his friends just to console them and cheer them up. The Jesus who appeared was the Good News to be proclaimed. So with the women running from the tomb (Matt. 28:10). So with the eleven on the appointed mountain in Galilee (Matt. 28:16–20). So with the eleven gathered on Easter evening (Luke 24:47–48). So with Mary Magdalen in the garden (John 20:17–18), with John's version of Easter evening (20:21), with Peter at the lakeside (21:15). So with Paul.

The vivid experience of the Spirit at Pentecost is described precisely as power and courage to do just that, to go out and proclaim salvation in and through the risen Lord. So—and this is the important conclusion from the whole structure of the evidence and apart from details—resurrection appearances and experience of the empowering Spirit, Easter and Pentecost, are inseparable. The Spirit of God at once reveals the risen Lord and gives power to proclaim him. This is one important feature about the evidence of Acts.

It seems clear that the first thing that happened was that Jesus' appearances to the first witnesses made them all gather together in Jerusalem eagerly expecting his return. John the Baptist and Jesus had both preached the imminent coming of the Kingdom of God. Jesus stands out in his lifetime as the prophet to end all prophets, the prophet of the last days. So the resurrection of Jesus was understood by the witnesses, not as an epilogue to his life, a crowning and rewarding and confirming of it by the Father, which men were to contemplate and believe in for years and centuries to come, but as the beginning of the End, the prelude to the general resurrection of believers (which in another sense it was). The tone of what seem to be the most primitive elements in Acts of how the Good News was first proclaimed is: The time is short: hurry up and believe, be converted, so that your sins get forgiven; for Jesus is about to come as Judge, and those who do not believe will be condemned. The Christian community was not at this time of animated expectation concerned to recall the life and teachings of Jesus or to draw up gospels. They first looked forward to the coming of the Risen One. Only by degrees did they then begin to look back, as the distance from the end of Jesus' life grew, and reflect on the whole meaning of Jesus, progressively recalling and understanding his life in terms of their belief in his resurrection and hope in his coming.

The second, and key, feature of the whole structure of the evidence of Acts is that the experience of being commissioned by the risen Jesus to preach the Good News *was* the experience of the Spirit poured out on them, seizing hold of them, giving them the message and the courage to proclaim it. This two-sided experience made them apostles. So with Paul, who claimed to be an apostle on the twofold ground that he had seen the Lord, and that Christ himself had instructed him and given him the message; he had not learned it from other men, however eminent in the Christian community (Gal. 1:11–12). This is the setting and meaning of Peter's first proclamation of the Gospel (Acts 2:4, 14–39; cf. 4:31), and of other 'speeches of proclamation' of varying length that are given in Acts.

It is for the most part implicit rather than explicit in Acts that the Spirit they experienced as seizing them was not just 'the' Spirit of God, given by God on behalf of Jesus, but the Spirit given by the risen Jesus himself. It is implicit in that they experienced being filled by God's Spirit (life-force and power) *in* being commissioned by the risen Jesus to proclaim him: they were aware of receiving 'his' Spirit. But it is sometimes also explicit: 'Being therefore exalted at (or by) the right hand of God, and having received from the Father the Holy Spirit, as was promised, *he has poured out* all that you see and hear,' namely the witnesses proclaiming the Gospel with vivid enthusiasm in languages they did not know (Acts 2:33). In the same way, the stories in Acts of the apostles exercising healing powers make it clear that it is the healing powers of Jesus, present by his Spirit (power) in the first community, that are being exercised by them. A good example is the cure of the cripple at the Beautiful Gate by Peter and John: the Jewish authorities ask them, ' "By what power or by what name (these are equivalent) have such men as you done this?" Then Peter filled with the Holy Spirit answered, ". . . it was by the name of Jesus of Nazareth . . ." ' (Acts 4:5–12).

What is mostly implicit in Acts is written on every page of Paul. His own conversion was an experience of the risen Jesus himself 'knocking him off his horse', instructing, commissioning, empowering him. For Paul 'spirit' is a pervasive word: it denotes first his own experience of God's power, and then that same experience in other Christians. This is a basic fact of his religion and his theology. And at all points this Spirit-power is explicitly identified as the power of the risen Christ, making him his apostle, founding the Church, present and active in believers and making them (an extension of) his risen body-self, and so sharers in his resurrection. A notable example is the passage in Romans where one should note the equivalences: (here italicized):

> You are on the spiritual level, if only *God's Spirit* dwells within you; and if a man does not possess the *Spirit of Christ*, he is no Christian. But if *Christ* is dwelling within you, then although the body is a dead thing because you sinned, yet the spirit is life itself because you have been justified. Moreover, if *the Spirit of him who raised Jesus from the dead* dwells within you, the God who raised Christ Jesus from the dead will also give new life to your mortal bodies through *his indwelling Spirit* (Rom. 8:9-11).

Compare Gal. 4:6, 'Because you are sons, God has sent the Spirit of his Son into your hearts.' But it is not so much a matter of examples as of the whole of his theology, based on his own experience of being seized by the risen Christ. It is important to stress that this theology is not for Paul a theorem, a pattern of thinking arising from putting ideas together; it is, as any sound theology is, an attempt to express his own religious experience and that of others. 'Spirit' is for him a power-word: the dynamic experience of being laid hold of, upheld and used by Christ: 'God's love has flooded our inmost hearts through the Holy Spirit he has given us' (Rom. 5:5).

All this is amply confirmed for the Christian communities as a whole from Paul's earliest letters. The 'charismata' (gifts) that were so manifest in the Pauline Churches—not ideas that were around, but tangible realities—*are* gifts, are the graces of God, in so far as they are the actions (energies, he says) of Christ's Spirit through the individual. They are not so much traits of character, permanent characteristics, as concrete events, actions made possible by the divine power. They are revelations and manifestations of the same Spirit who dwells (this word does denote permanence) in all. His own original preaching at Corinth was an instance of 'demonstrating the Spirit's power' (I Cor. 2:4). Speaking in tongues, one of the charismatic gifts which Paul wishes to put in its place, is obviously an action or event; but so are the other gifts he speaks of (I Cor. 12), such as the gift of wise speech, putting the deepest knowledge into words, faith (a mountain-moving, manifest faith), healing, miraculous powers, revealing utterances, testing such utterances; so are faith and hope and love, the greatest gifts of all. The Christian communities experienced the power of the risen Christ among them, transforming their whole lives. And this enabling power of Christ formed them into a single fellowship, community, body; a community of faith and hope, bound together in love. The unity was itself tangible.

It can be the scholar's mistake to imagine that the thinking about Jesus developed among the early Christians by a purely cerebral process, one idea leading to another, being fed by words heard and read. It has been admirably remarked that scholars tend to create evangelists in their own image and likeness. They tend to imagine the Gospels taking shape at the hands of men sitting at their desks, piecing together various bits of documentation, elaborating them by reference to Old Testament passages, with constant reference to their bookshelf of rabbinic theology and other contemporary or ancient publications. It is an easy mistake, but a serious one none the less. It overlooks the real task of theology (as opposed to biblical scholarship), which is to give expression to today's religious experience in a process of interaction between 'the tradition', the received material and practices, and what Christian life is actually like when lived in the here-and-now world. Of course, in searching for adequate expression of that lived experience, the Christian (or any) writer can only use available and recognizable languages and the religious experiences that they in turn evoke. So for the later scholar to trace the literary genesis of the developing theologies may be to say precious little about their value and meanings to the people who formed them. What Paul was writing about was the vivid and concrete experience of himself and his Christian communities, knocked off their horses of orthodox Judaism or of gentile religions by the tangible power of the risen Christ.

To summarize. For those who saw the Lord, the resurrection appearances and the vivid experience of the outpouring of the Spirit are interlocked in such a way that they recognize the Spirit with which (or with whom) they are filled as the Spirit of God sent them by the risen Christ, indeed as Christ's way of continuing through them his life of mediating salvation by word and deed.

Those who did not see the Lord and yet believed in his resurrection did so both because they witnessed the manifestations of the Spirit's powers in word and deed through the witnesses, and because they themselves experienced the power which they heard proclaimed as the power of the risen Christ, present and active within them and among them. The powerful proclamation of the message and visible manifestations associated with it enabled them to interpret or to 'know' interiorly the Spirit active in themselves, and among them as a group, as the risen Christ's Spirit.

One of the many threads running through John's gospel is a theology of faith in terms of 'seeing' and 'believing'. We catch the meaning when we realize that these words make a contrast between seeing merely physically and seeing spiritually, that is seeing with the eyes of the Spirit and therefore seeing what God is communicating, i.e. believing. The Gospel, it says, was written 'that you may (come to) believe that Jesus is the Christ, the Son of God, and that through this faith you may possess life in his name (by his power)' (20:31). The Gospel leads up to the story of Thomas and to the punch-line, 'Because you have seen me you have believed (or, Have you believed because you have seen me?). Blessed are those who did not see and believed' (20:29).

Like other themes in John, this one operates on three levels. There is the literal and earthy level of those who only saw (materially), like Nicodemus, or the Pharisees, so hostile to the man cured of blindness from birth (9:35–41). There is the 'really seeing' or believing level of the man born blind, who ends up seeing not merely physically but also spiritually, or of Thomas when he recognized the man who addressed him: both call Jesus 'Lord'. Another example is that of those who saw and those who did not see (6:35–36) that Jesus was himself the bread of life, the bread from heaven. And then there is the third level in all this of what John is saying to his own local Church: they are not to bemoan the fact that they were not eye-witnesses to Jesus either alive or risen; they are blessed by God to see truly, to believe.

John's and Paul's theologies of the Spirit differ in some points but are the same in many basic ways. For both, the gift of the Spirit is the risen Lord's way of dwelling (abiding) in the believer and giving him life (John 4:10–14; 7:37–39; and the passages about abiding in Chapter 17). The risen Christ gives them *his* Spirit (he breathes on them) to make them the community of apostles (those he sends) and the community of forgiveness or reconciliation with God (John 2:21–23). Because God abides in them, they must be united, a community. Jesus promises the Paraclete, a word of some four different meanings all of which John uses (interpreter and teacher, witness, advocate with the Father, consoler and strengthener): compare Paul's charismata. After Jesus' departure, the Spirit will lead them into all truth: he will guide them to see the true meaning of Jesus. Like Paul, John means by 'spirit' not an idea but an experience, the characteristic Christian experience of Spirit: only this explains the otherwise puzzling saying of John:'This he said of the Spirit those who believed in him were going to receive: for there was as yet no Spirit, because Jesus had not yet been glorified' (7:39). John did not mean that the Spirit did not yet exist, but that the spring had not yet come.

6

THE DIVINITY OF CHRIST

The early Christians did not think of the Spirit in later 'ontological' terms, speculating about his being: for them he was what he did; they knew him as the life-force of the risen Christ, given by the Father, enabling them to see truly, to preach, to have courage, even to cure. Similarly they asked functional questions about Jesus (what is his role in God's plan for man?), and did not ask or answer questions about the constitution of his being. What was certain and obvious from the start was that he was a man like themselves.

It was later generations of Christians, living in a world where education was along the lines of Greek philosophy, and having to give an account of their belief in such a world, who asked the more speculative questions. Was this man just a great prophet, the prophet to end all prophets and to deliver God's final message, a human instrument of God who was almost in a class by himself? Or was he more than that, and some sort of intermediary being between God and man? Or was he somehow to be identified with the being of God himself? All the Christian witnesses who produced the New Testament were monotheists of Jewish origin (as was Jesus), whose cardinal principle of religion was that there is only One God. You cannot even ask whether the man Jesus is somehow to be identified with God until you have in some way begun to differentiate the One God. The process is well on its way in Paul's letter to the Romans and in the Gospel of John. Succeeding

Christian generations in a Greek milieu struggled to answer the new questions with which they were faced by cross-questioning the witness of New Testament writers who had not been thinking in these terms. In doing so they leant so heavily on the Gospel of John, with its doctrine of the Word (or Wisdom) of God made flesh, that they virtually excluded the many other ways of thinking about Jesus that are apparent in the New Testament. Eventually (451 AD), after centuries of often bitter controversy, the Council of Chalcedon defined that Jesus was truly God and truly man, not some strange mixture of the two, but one divine person (possessor of a nature) in two natures, the nature (or inner essential constituents) of God and of man.

No thought pattern is going to be adequate, and the two centuries after Chalcedon showed that a very large proportion of Christians indeed were much dissatisfied with this one. However, it prevailed in the even longer run, after further clarifications. In our own time the formula of Chalcedon has been much criticized—though by no means always understood by its critics, or properly assimilated by the centuries which followed it. Chalcedon teaches that being God made Jesus more of a true man, not less; and conversely that it was precisely his real and particular humanness as 'this man Jesus' (Acts 2:36) that expressed and conveyed the very God-head of God. But later centuries of devotion, largely in continuing reaction against the Arianism of some of the Germanic tribes which swamped Europe, gradually deserted Chalcedon in their actual religion while affirming it in their doctrinal formulas, and produced an image of Jesus that was almost wholly divine and hardly human. The qualities of the divine nature came to be attributed to the human nature, such as omniscience (clean contrary to Chalcedon): Jesus in his lifetime, indeed in his cradle, knew everything (astrophysics etc.) but did not let on; he knew in advance all that was to come about; he could not possibly be in error about who wrote the Psalms; when he said he did not know when the End would come (Mark 13:32), he could not of course have meant what he said, etc. We have all inherited this picture. One fault in it is that it has a static or timeless picture of Jesus, leaving no room for human development through life and beyond it; it attributes all the qualities of the risen, exalted and glorified Christ to the mortal Jesus.

So, very properly, there has been a reaction in our time: a reaction of starting from the real humanness of Jesus and working from there; an insistence that he was not an ideal man but a Jew, of his own time, limited in all the ways that a man is limited by his sex, his make-up, his time, his people. Today, and this is the task of theology in every age, we have to reassimilate Chalcedon in terms of our own concrete human world. And in that world it is not sufficient, in Greek mode, to be satisfied with saying that Jesus was truly human because all the parts going to make up the essence of man were there: body, soul, memory, understanding, will, imagination, etc. In our world part of what it is to be human is to experience life the way we do: to grow in knowledge of God, of life, of oneself; to be uncertain, insecure and sometimes anxious about ultimate realities and one's human future; to have to pick one's way through life. And that is what is meant by the Word becoming 'flesh': one of us, fragile, dependent, vulnerable, mortal, and limited in knowledge as well as everything else one could describe from a secular point of view. Which does not exclude the idea that only Jesus lived human life as God meant it to be lived and was in that sense more a man than any of us. But it does exclude the idea that he was 'perfect' in irrelevant (and even unintelligible) senses.

Inevitably, with this approach of understanding Jesus 'from below' rather than 'from above', and in the context of biblical studies, questions have been asked about the growth in understanding of Jesus among early Christians. There certainly was a growth. There is a great distance between what Peter is reported to have said of the risen Christ, 'God has made this man Jesus, whom you crucified, both Lord and Messiah' (Acts

2:36), implying that he was not Lord or Messiah in his lifetime, and the divine figure of the Word made flesh in John's Gospel, and beyond that to the great figure of the cosmic Christ in the later Pauline letters (Ephesians and Colossians). It should not surprise us that there was a growth in Christian understanding and expression; there must have been a growth; there is no reason for thinking that all the truth about Jesus must or could have been grasped from the beginning. Indeed, has it all been grasped yet? It should not surprise or shock us if elements of the 'proclamation speeches' in Acts seem 'primitive' and do not bear witness to the divinity of Jesus even in his risen and glorified state: see Acts 3:2–26; 5:29–32; 10:34–43; 13:26–41. Whereas there are parts of other speeches that go somewhat further: Acts 2:33; 4:8–12. Only in John can it be said that Jesus is directly called 'God', though it is implied in some passages in the New Testament letters. As has been said, you first have to learn to differentiate 'God'. Jesus was certainly not Jahweh, the Father, creator of heaven and earth. But what *validates* the development? There are grounds for saying that the earliest Christian belief was that Jesus was a man raised by God from the dead and appointed Judge of all men (Acts 10:42). What grounds were there for going beyond that?

The resurrection witnesses proclaimed, 'I have seen *the Lord*.' They grasped the risen Jesus from the outset as 'the Lord'. The earliest confession of Christian faith we have is the simple 'Jesus (Christ) is Lord.' This is the primitive creed: Rom. 10:9 ('If on your lips is the confession "Jesus is Lord" and in your heart the faith that God raised him from the dead, then you will find salvation'); I Cor. 12:3; 2 Cor. 4:5; Phil. 2:11; and passages in Acts already referred to. But what did the title 'Lord' *mean* to the earliest Christians? This is not at all the same as asking from what various secular or religious vocabularies they might have drawn it. The question is how they used it.

We have got so used to speaking of Jesus as 'Our Lord' that

it has for us lost its specific meaning; just as for Paul 'Christ' has almost always become simply a surname and has lost its specific meaning of 'the Messiah', because this was a meaning he could never convey to gentile converts. The special sense of Lord is 'he who has mastery over all the powers that hold the human world in thrall'. The hymn in Phil. 2:6–11 is pre-Pauline and so very 'primitive': the name given to Jesus is LORD, a name throughout Paul's writings applied to the risen Christ, not to the mortal Jesus (which corresponds to Acts 2:36, 'God has made him both Lord and Messiah'); 'name' means 'power' as this hymn shows; God has bestowed on him the name that is above all names, that at the name (Lord) of Jesus every knee should bow, in heaven, on earth and in the depths; he has power over all powers. In fact in using these phrases the hymn is quoting Isa. 45:23 and saying of the risen Jesus what is there said of God. But the Old Testament text most consistently quoted or referred to in connection with Jesus' becoming Lord in his exaltation is Ps. 110(109):1, understood as meaning, 'The Lord (God) said to my Lord (the risen Christ), "Sit on my right, while I make your enemies the footstool under your feet." ' So, in Acts 2:34–36 and other places. God has given him power over all powers that threaten men, even the last enemy, death. The idea is worked out in full in I Cor. 15:23–28. In his lifetime Jesus preached the Kingdom of his Father, but was not hailed as king, except by Pilate, who so understood the title 'Messiah' which the crowds pressed on Jesus, and perhaps by the crowd in John 6:15. (The evangelists like the irony of Pilate hailing him 'king', because in his death and resurrection he really did become Messiah as God intended.) In his resurrection God makes the world his kingdom, so that he may subject the world and himself to God. To sit at the right hand of God (on his throne) means to share his power: it is the pictorial image that corresponds to the images of resurrection, exaltation, glorification (sharing the splendour of God).

So the title 'Lord' given to the risen Jesus, in conjunction with Ps. 110 (109):1, shows that *from the beginning* the risen Jesus was seen as sharing the power (Spirit) of God and dispensing it to creation, in particular as salvation to those believing in him, but beyond that in a lordship over all creation, which included in the thought of the time the 'angelic' forces of good and evil. And this is precisely what they *experienced* in the outpouring of the Spirit.

Hence the christological developments are not just the growing fancy of writers, teachers, or bookish men. They are the attempt to penetrate and to express more fully this basic and original resurrection faith. From Easter onwards the spiritual vision of the witnesses was that Jesus was risen and that *he* was communicating to them in abundance the Spirit or life-force of God. By degrees the plain implication of this fact was spelled out: he was sharing the life-force of God with God, seeing that he was sharing it with them.

One way of understanding this was bound to be the idea that Jesus, a mere man though specially inspired by God for a unique role, was raised, exalted and glorified by God and adopted by God as Son into his own life (the process was seen as starting at the baptism of Jesus by John); the man 'became God', except that you have to start differentiating God before you can even try to think that. This 'adoptionism' is ultimately unintelligible and was condemned by the Church. But we have to distinguish developments in the minds of Christians from developments in the status and being of Jesus. Obviously, in the understanding of those who were first introduced to Jesus by John the Baptist, he progressively 'became God'. The heresy of adoptionism is after New Testament times, and involves asking questions about the being of Jesus and answering that his being started as human and became divine. Adoptionism is the opposite of the understanding already at least sketched in the Philippian (pre–Pauline) hymn, and made explicit by John, that God became this man. The thought–model of John was the one used by the Church to define the classic doctrine of the incarnation: however, it has the disadvantage of obscuring or leading one to overlook the fact that there was a development, not only in Jesus' ordinary human growth to maturity, but in his salvific *roles*. Adoptionism, wrong though it is in the question it is answering, at least prevents one from saying everything about the living Jesus, at all points in his life, that is true of the risen Christ. Because he was a real man, and because in the sense suggested he was more of a man than anyone else, Jesus progressively developed throughout his life his own conscious relationship with the Father, and his own understanding of the role the Father laid on him as saviour: at some point in his public life he realized his mission was from a human point of view going to be a failure; there is no reason for thinking he knew this at the outset. And orthodoxy about the being of Jesus does not demand that at the end of his life his understanding of the Father's will for him was perfectly developed; if the person possessing or constituting his humanity was divine, the humanity is nevertheless totally human. In a true sense, if one thinks in terms of role and function as New Testament writers did, he progressively became the Son of God in the obedience of his life and death, the complete attuning of himself to the Father in the changing concrete circumstances of his life. In this perspective he became Lord in his resurrection-exaltation, and disposed then of the Spirit and power of God in a way in which he did not in his lifetime (John 7:39; Acts 2:36). He became Messiah, Christ, in his exaltation, as Christian faith understood the title, and not as it was understood in his lifetime by the crowds, by Pilate, and indeed by his own followers. He became Servant. And in one set of meanings attached to the title, he is yet to become Son of Man: the Christian people awaits his coming.

7

OUR FAITH

So, why do *we* believe? We asked the question of the first believers who had not themselves 'seen the Lord', and now we are in a position to ask it of ourselves.

In New Testament times nearly everyone came to Christian faith from 'outside', first from Jewish faith and then from the varying religious and secular backgrounds that were scattered round Greece and the eastern provinces of the Roman Empire. But increasingly, since those first generations, Christians have been born into the Church; and that will be true of most readers of this book. We derived our faith gradually from our mothers and fathers, as they said prayers with us, showed us pictures and illustrated booklets, took us to church, explained statues, lit candles; we entered more deeply and personally into it in the company of the wider family, parish, school; we began to know something of the New and Old Testaments from parents, clergy, teachers; we related it all more or less successfully to the rest of life, as it developed and we developed.

The earliest believers who had not themselves seen the Lord in his lifetime or in his resurrection appearances believed because they experienced the risen Lord present, powerful and active in their midst, namely, both in their own hearts and in the believing community around them, with whom they were one. This experience or life was itself spread and passed on to succeeding generations, interpreted all along by 'the tradition', that is by the apostolic witness to the living, crucified and risen

Jesus, and by the whole practice of the Christian communities, in particular their celebration of Baptism and the Eucharist. They did not merely pass on documents or ideas but a corporate life: the Way, Luke calls it. Subsequent generations have entered into and shared this corporate life in the Spirit, nourished by the sacraments and the apostolic witness, down to our own day. We believe for the same reasons, on the same grounds, as have all believers who did not themselves see the Lord. Every generation has had the task of relating the tradition of writings and practice to their own culture, age, civilization, human world, ever changing and developing. Every generation has had to reappropriate and re-express the tradition by a process of interaction between the received Way and the insights, problems, perspectives, discoveries, qualities, concerns, of their own age. The fact that in each time and place 'the faith', in its wholeness, has sustained, illuminated, and made ultimate sense of human life in all its varieties, has built up a great wealth of corporate experience, corporate vision and awareness, corporate knowledge, one dares to say, which itself in its own way confirms and validates the faith.

We need to focus intensely and sharply on the fact that faith rests and is grounded on encountering God as he addresses himself to us in human life, and Christian faith on encountering God as he communicates 'his-self' in Christ. We can only have faith in a person, and then only if we meet him. We do not meet Jesus as Peter and James and John did in Galilee. But nor did Paul. And in those days in Galilee, though the basis of a personal devotion to Jesus was laid, making it possible for his followers to proclaim the same Jesus, living, crucified and risen, they had not yet come to specifically Christian faith. We encounter the risen Christ, as he now is and where he now is, living and manifesting himself in the community that lives and follows the Way, by the power of his Spirit. We encounter him principally and centrally in people: people close to us; people we love and people we revere; holy people; people we hear about who inspire us, the saints; and all of them people guided and nourished by the Scriptures and leading us back to them. We encounter Christ in the Eucharist in a special relationship: in the Eucharist his presence and saving action in his body the Church are further embodied as food and drink and conveyed to us. We are able to know him there, where he is, in his body the Church, because we share the same Spirit who gives us eyes to see.

If it may still seem somehow tenuous to assert so firmly that we truly meet and know the risen Christ as he dwells by his Spirit in the Church, even when we recall that faith is an obscure vision, like a vision of the heart, we should reflect again on Paul's assertion that Jesus has become life-giving Spirit (I Cor. 15:45). Since his resurrection Jesus can be known by men only as life-giving Spirit. But he has also become the last Adam, the New Man, and it is precisely in and among this new race of men that he is to be encountered. Further, he is the Son, not the Father: he did not preach his Kingdom but his Father's; he is the way, not the goal. To have Christian faith is not ultimately to meet Christ and to know Christ, but to recognize and respond to the Father, who communicates himself through the Son in the Spirit. It was the hearth and heart of Jewish religion to believe that God was in their midst, and his presence was specially symbolized and realized in the Temple: John alludes to this when he says that the eternal Word 'pitched his tent (tabernacled) among us'. But Christians need no temple, no building, for '*We* are the temple of the living God' (2 Cor. 6:16); 'the temple of God is holy, and that temple you are' (I Cor. 3:17).

In his lifetime the question was put to Jesus, 'By what authority do you do these things?' His followers, even if they could not then recognize him as God become man, were those who were able to recognize as present in him in a unique way the 'authority', the power in word and deed of God, bringing salvation. We may put the same question to ourselves and to the

Church; 'By what authority did the early Church develop its understanding and its proclamation of Jesus living, crucified and risen? By what authority has the Church throughout the centuries interpreted the apostolic witness and striven to answer the questions put to that witness by succeeding ages and civilizations?' We cannot answer these questions simply by tracing the growth and interaction of thought patterns. They cannot be answered from without, but only from within, the circle of faith. We can answer them only by sharing deeply in the corporate Christian experience, and coming there face to face with the Father who gives us his life through the Son. Paul ends his second letter to the Corinthians with the blessing, familiar to us all, in which he expresses in three ways this one reality of experience: 'The grace of our Lord Jesus Christ, and the love of God, and the fellowship of the Holy Spirit, be with you all evermore.'

FURTHER READING

John Coventry, S.J., *The Theology of Faith*. Cork, Mercier Press, 1968.

Gerald O'Collins, S.J., *Theology and Revelation*. Cork, Mercier Press, 1968.

John Coventry, S.J., *Christian Truth*. London, Darton, Longman & Todd, 1975.

Bruce Vawter, *This Man Jesus*. London, Geoffrey Chapman, 1975.

Dermot A. Lane, *The Reality of Jesus*. Dublin, Veritas Publications, 1975.

Gerald O'Collins, S.J., *Has Dogma a Future?* London, Darton, Longman & Todd, 1975.

Practical Theology Series
Edited by Edmund Flood and John Coventry

Today's Catholic
Edmund Flood, O.S.B.
(Introductory Volume)

Faith in Jesus Christ
John Coventry, S.J.

The Church
David Morland, O.S.B.

God
David Morland, O.S.B.

Married Life
Vincent Nichols

Divorce Problems Today for Catholics
Kevin Kelly and Jack Dominian

Moral Decisions
Gerard Hughes, S.J.

Parish and Worship
Anthony Bullen, Brian Newns and others

Teaching the Faith
Gerard Rummery, F.S.C. and Damian Lundy, F.S.C.

Christian Leadership
Edmund Jones, O.S.B.

Is Ours a Just World?
Valentine Fitzgerald

The Role of Women in the Church
Oliver and Ianthe Pratt and Peter and Patricia Worden